VOCAL SELECTIONS

Stage Entertainment USA & Sylvester Stallone
Metro-Goldwyn-Mayer
The Shubert Organization   Kevin King-Templeton
James L. Nederlander & Terry Allen Kramer   Roy Furman   Chery
Zane Tankel   Lucky Champions   Scott Delman   JFL Theatricals /
Latitude Link   Waxman / Shin / Bergère   Lauren Stevens / Jo:

PRESENT

ROCKY

BOOK BY
Thomas Meehan and Sylvester Stallone

MUSIC BY
Stephen Flaherty

LYRICS BY
Lynn Ahrens

Based on the MGM / United Artists Motion Picture

STARRING

Andy Karl

Margo Seibert   Terence Archie

AND

Dakin Matthews   Danny Mastrogiorgio   Jennifer Mudge

WITH

Eric Anderson   Adrian Aguilar   Michelle Aravena   James Brown III   Sam J. Cahn   Vincent Corazza   Kevin Del Aguila
Ned Eisenberg   Bradley Gibson   Stacey Todd Holt   Sasha Hutchings   David Andrew Macdonald   Vasthy Mompoint
Vince Oddo   Okieriete Onaodowan   Adam Perry   Kristin Piro   Luis Salgado   John Schiappa   Samantha Shafer
Wallace Smith   Jenny Lee Stern   Dan'yelle Williamson   Mark Zimmerman

SCENIC DESIGN
Christopher Barreca

COSTUME DESIGN
David Zinn

LIGHTING DESIGN
Christopher Akerlind

SOUND DESIGN
Peter Hylenski

VIDEO DESIGN
Dan Scully
Pablo N. Molina

SPECIAL EFFECTS DESIGN
Jeremy Chernick

WIG & MAKE-UP DESIGN
Harold Mertens

CASTING
Jim Carnahan, CSA
Carrie Gardner, CSA

MUSIC SUPERVISOR
David Holcenberg

ORCHESTRATIONS
Stephen Trask
Doug Besterman

MUSIC DIRECTOR
Chris Fenwick

VOCAL ARRANGEMENTS
Stephen Flaherty

MUSIC COORDINATOR
John Miller

PRODUCTION STAGE MANAGER
Lisa Dawn Cave

PRESS REPRESENTATIVE
Polk & Co.

ADVERTISING / MARKETING
SpotCo

ASSOCIATE PRODUCERS
Barbara Darwall
Michael Hildebrandt

EXECUTIVE PRODUCERS
Adam Silberman
Eric Cornell

VP MARKETING & COMMUNICATIONS
Michele Groner

PRODUCTION SUPERVISORS
Jake Bell
Lily Twining

GENERAL MANAGER
Bespoke Theatricals

PRODUCERS
Joop van den Ende and Bill Taylor

CHOREOGRAPHY BY
Steven Hoggett & Kelly Devine

DIRECTED BY
Alex Timbers

World Premiere at the TUI Operettenhaus, Hamburg, Germany

Production Photography: Matthew Murphy
Cover Art: Nigel Parry/CPi

ISBN 978-1-4803-8701-0

HAL•LEONARD®
CORPORATION

7777 W. BLUEMOUND RD. P.O. BOX 13819 MILWAUKEE, WI 53213

In Australia Contact:
Hal Leonard Australia Pty. Ltd.
4 Lentara Court
Cheltenham, Victoria, 3192 Australia
Email: ausadmin@halleonard.com.au

Andy Karl, Dakin Matthews

Margo Seibert

Andy Karl

Andy Karl

Margo Seibert, Andy Karl

Kristin Piro, Terence Archie, Sasha Hutchings

Wallace Smith,
Terence Archie,
Andy Karl,
David Macdonald

ROCKY

BROADWAY

AIN'T DOWN YET

Lyrics by LYNN AHRENS
Music by STEPHEN FLAHERTY

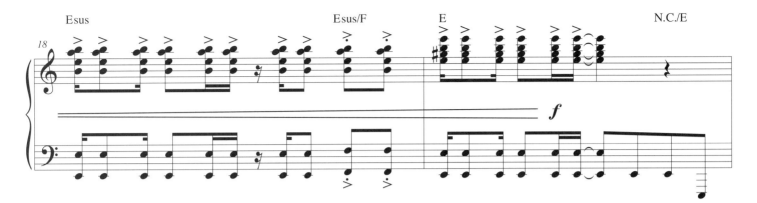

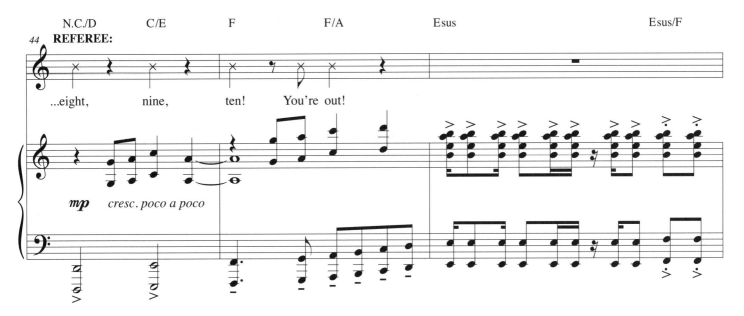

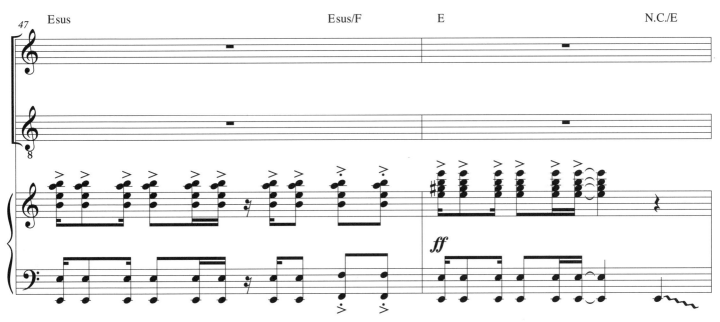

MY NOSE AIN'T BROKEN

Lyrics by LYNN AHRENS
Music by STEPHEN FLAHERTY

Simple and flowing, in "2" (♩ = 100)

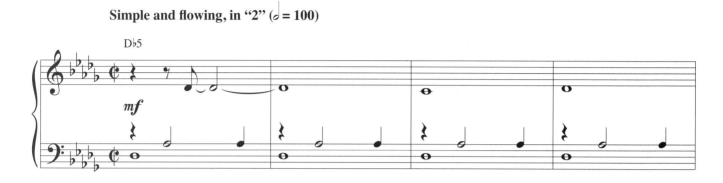

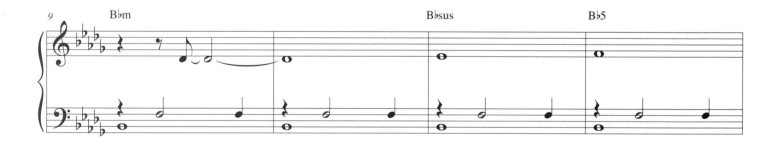

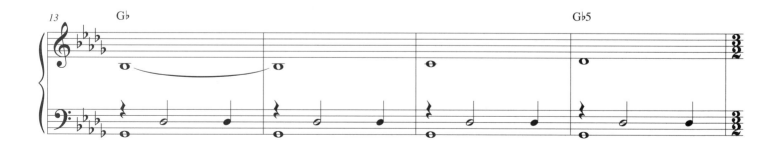

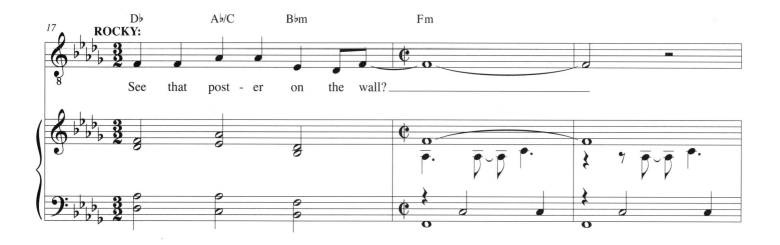

ROCKY: See that post-er on the wall?

Rock-y Mar-ci-a - no. Nev-er took a sin-gle

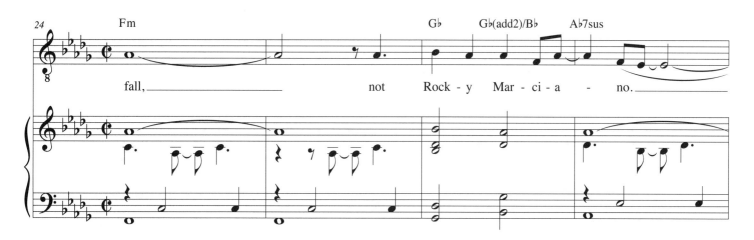

fall, not Rock-y Mar-ci-a - no.

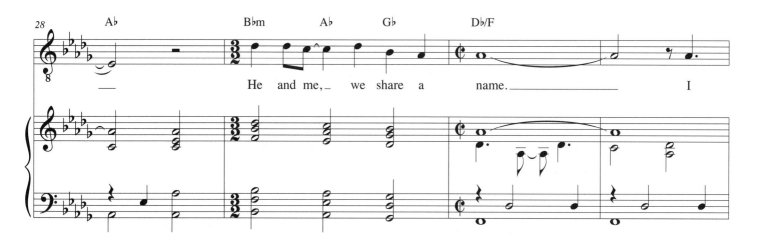

He and me, we share a name. I

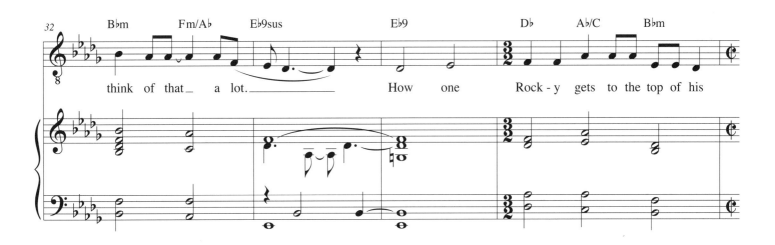

think of that_ a lot._ How one Rock - y gets to the top of his

game_ and the oth - er Rock - y_ gets what I_

_ got._

I got ten sore knuck - les and a ring - in' ear. I got a

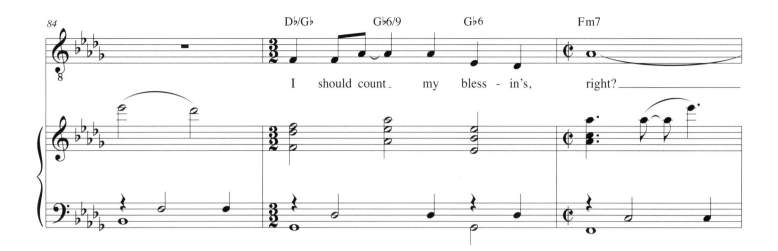

I should count my bless - in's, right?

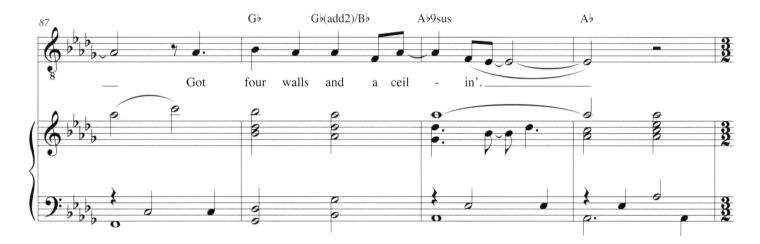

Got four walls and a ceil - in'.

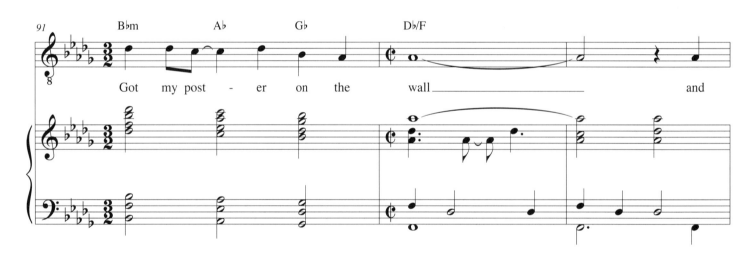

Got my post - er on the wall and

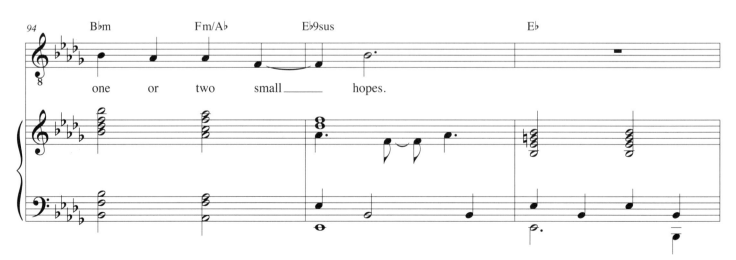

one or two small hopes.

RAINING

Lyrics by LYNN AHRENS
Music by STEPHEN FLAHERTY

With movement (♩ = 94)

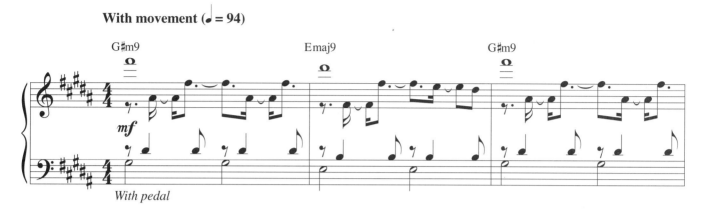

ADRIAN:
Watch him turn__ his col-lar up__ a-gainst the__ wet.

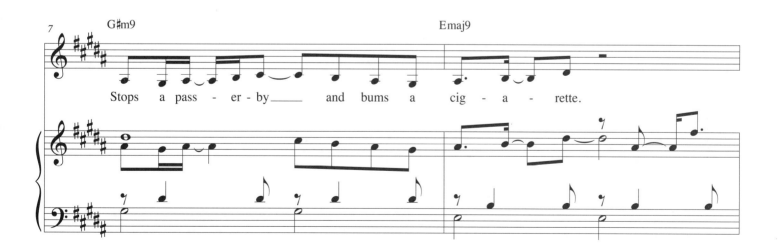

Stops a pass-er-by____ and bums a cig-a-rette.

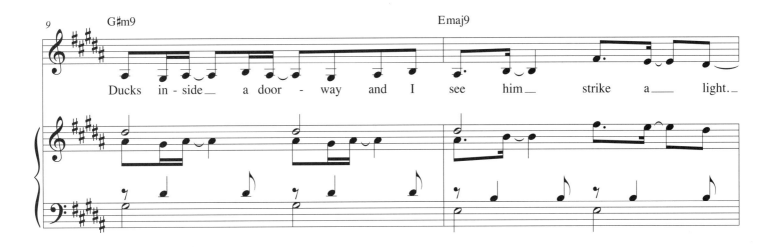

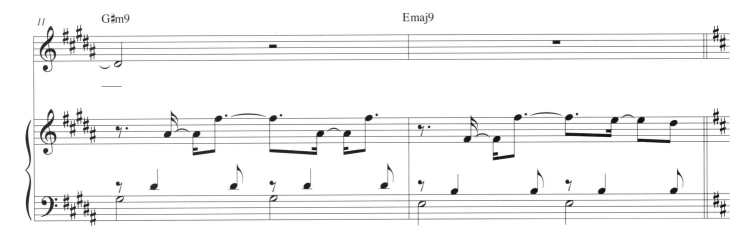

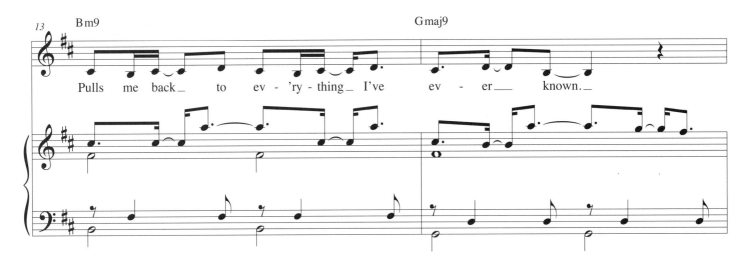

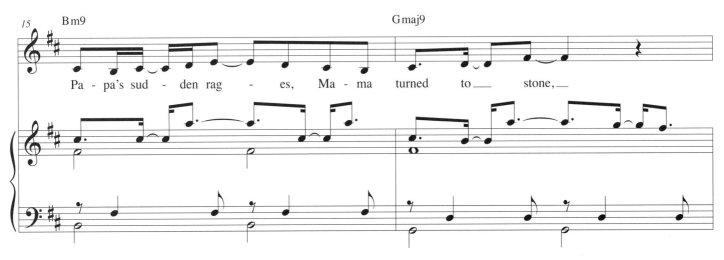

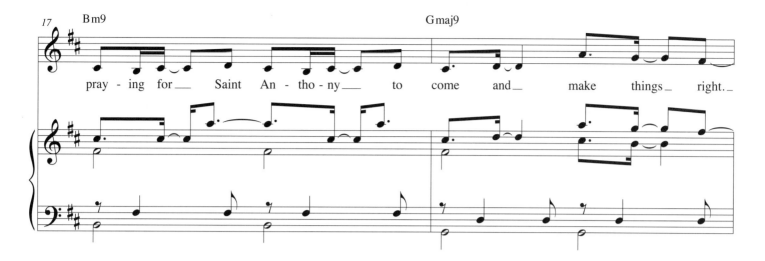

pray - ing for __ Saint An - tho - ny __ to come and __ make things __ right. __

You

don't look up and you don't talk back and your odds are ten __ to none, like a

weed that grows from a pave - ment crack toward a patch of sun. You

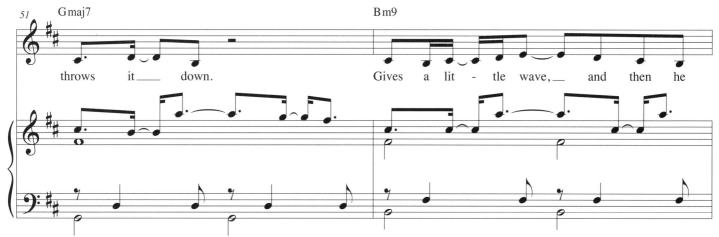

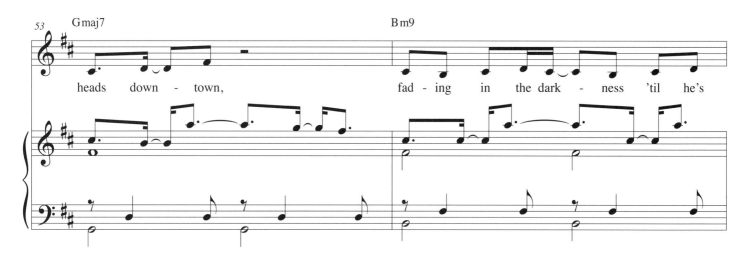

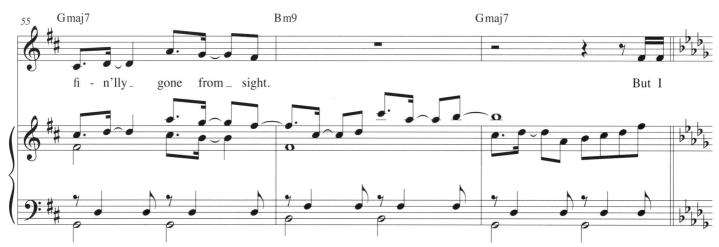

PATRIOTIC

Lyrics by LYNN AHRENS
Music by STEPHEN FLAHERTY

Freely, with bravado

APOLLO: Now here's what's go - in' down.__ Gon-na say it just__ one__ time.__ On Jan-u-ar-y first, nine-teen-sev-en-ty-six. I'm_____ gon-na

* Bars 1–15 were cut from the Broadway production.

who the hell in Phil - ly do we got? Bil - ly Snow? Rhymes __

__ with no! __ Big Chuck Krull? Too old, __ too dull. Dip - per

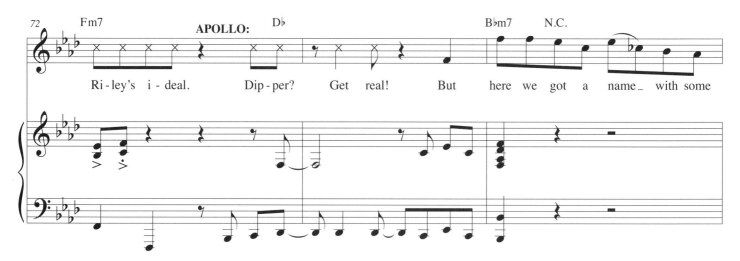

Ri - ley's i - deal. Dip - per? Get real! But here we got a name __ with some

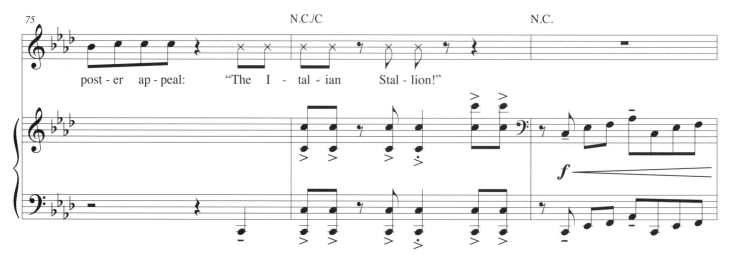

post - er ap - peal: "The I - tal - ian Stal - lion!"

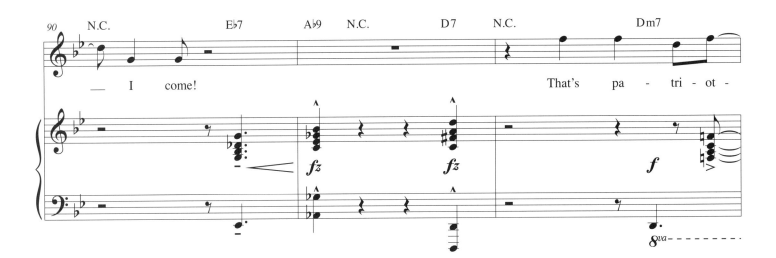

APOLLO: *Apollo Creed meets the Italian Stallion. Shit! Sounds like a damn monster movie!*

THE FLIP SIDE

Lyrics by LYNN AHRENS
Music by STEPHEN FLAHERTY

ROCKY:
You wan - na skate. I'm gon - na watch____ ya. If

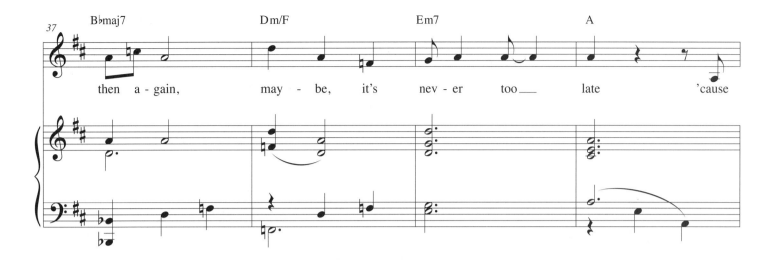

then a - gain, may - be, it's nev - er too____ late 'cause

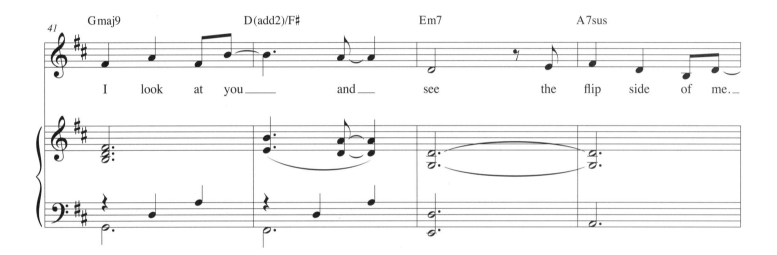

I look at you____ and____ see the flip side of me.____

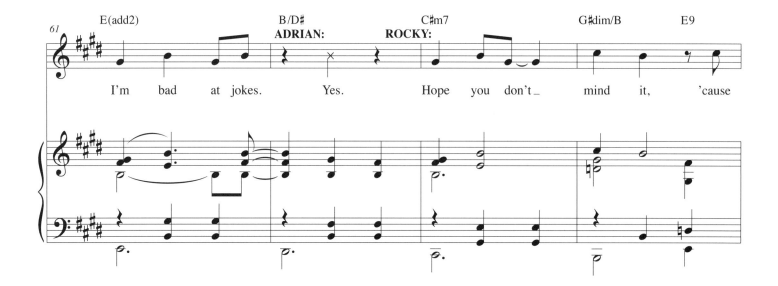

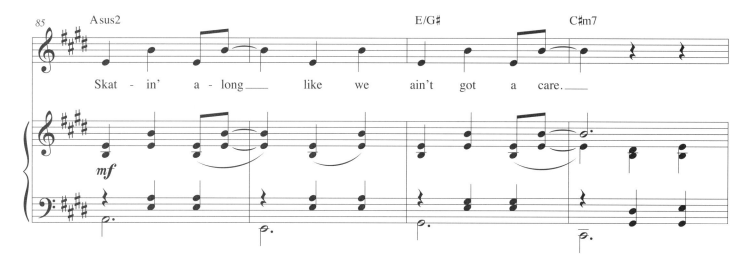

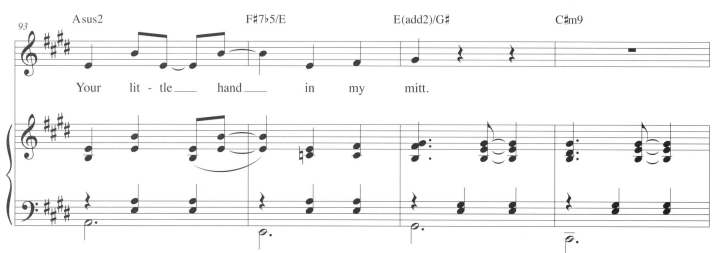

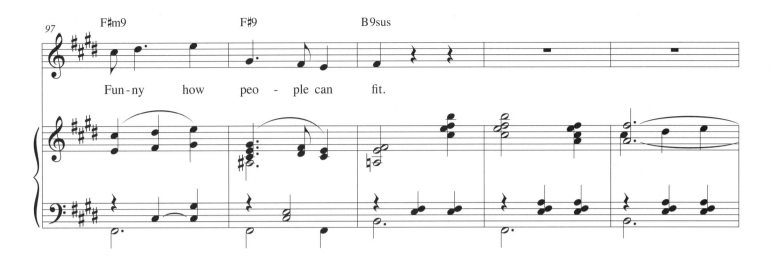

Fun - ny how peo - ple can fit.

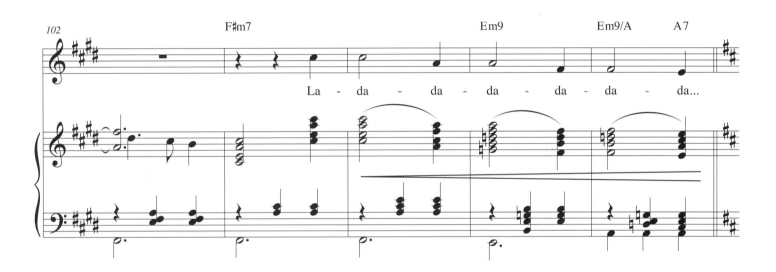

La - da - da - da - da - da - da...

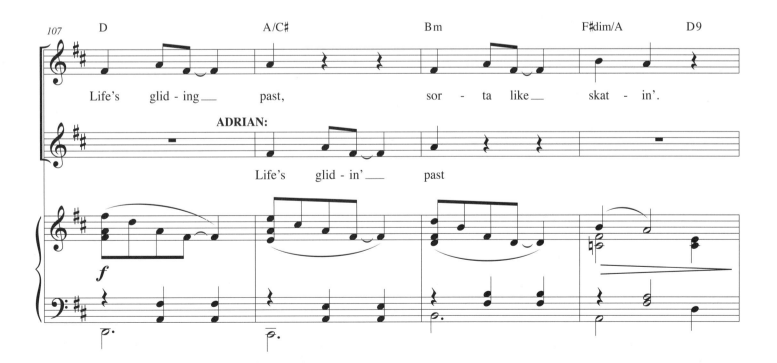

Life's glid - ing___ past, sor - ta like___ skat - in'.

ADRIAN:

Life's glid - in'___ past

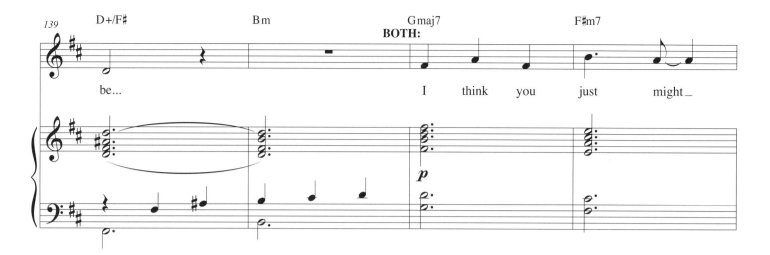

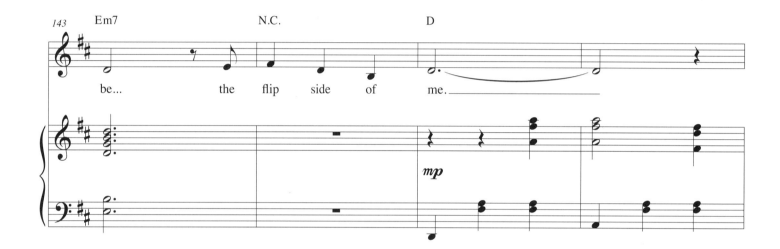

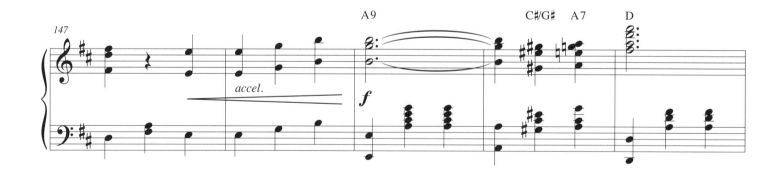

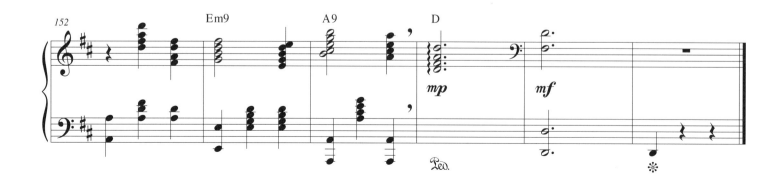

ADRIAN

Lyrics by LYNN AHRENS
Music by STEPHEN FLAHERTY

FIGHT FROM THE HEART

Lyrics by LYNN AHRENS
Music by STEPHEN FLAHERTY

Moderately, with heart (♩. = 67)

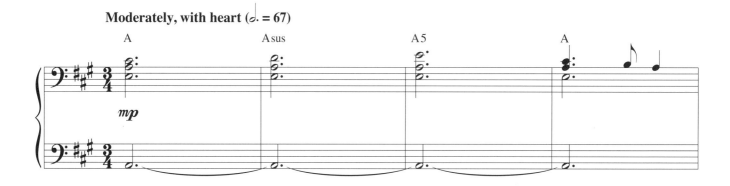

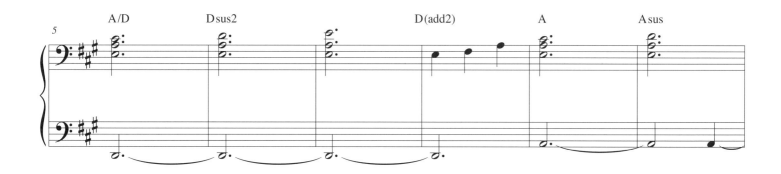

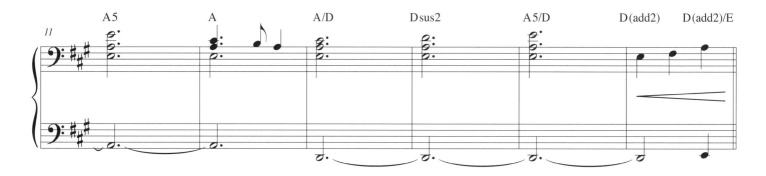

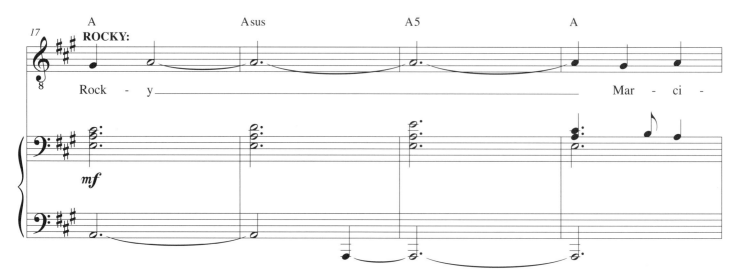

Rock - y _____ Mar - ci -

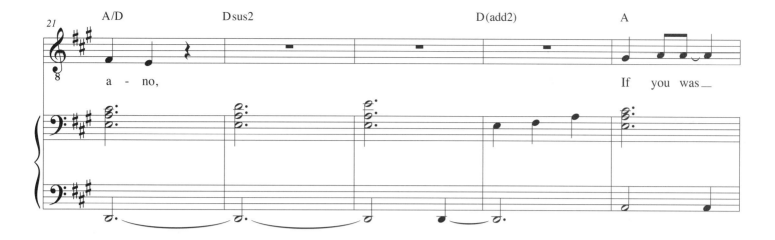

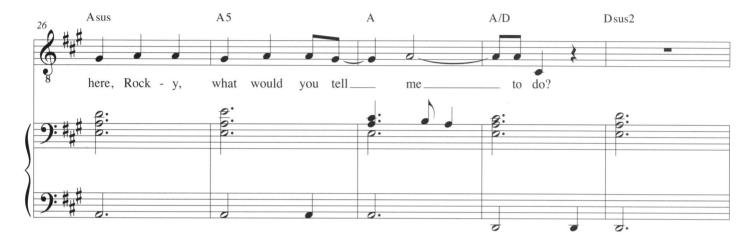

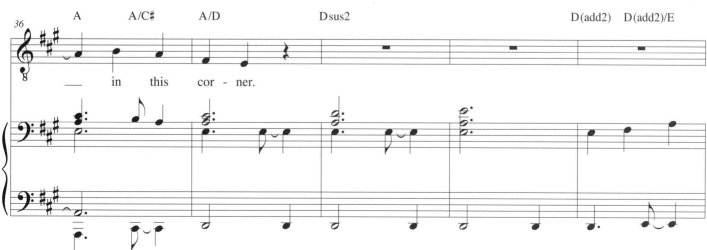

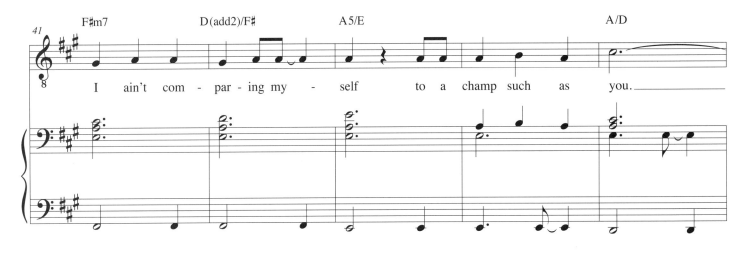

I ain't com - par - ing my - self to a champ such as you.

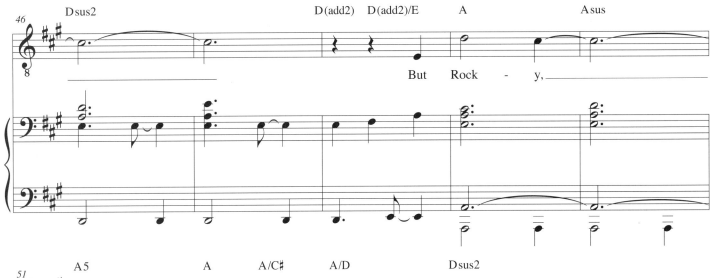

But Rock - y,

you been through it.

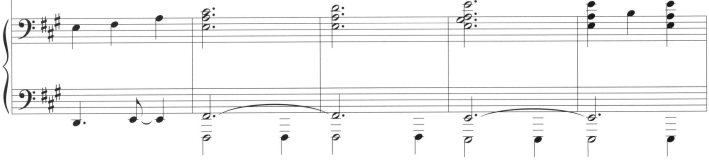

Mak - in' the choice of your life in a sec - ond or

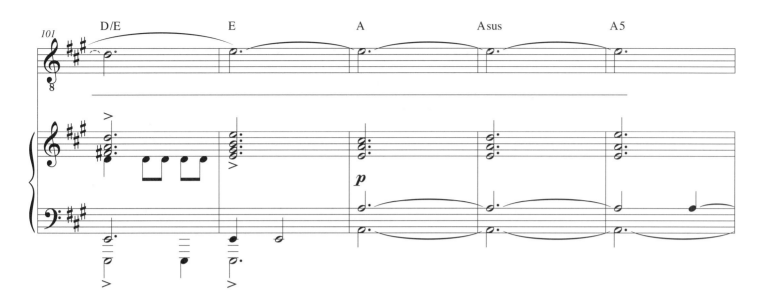

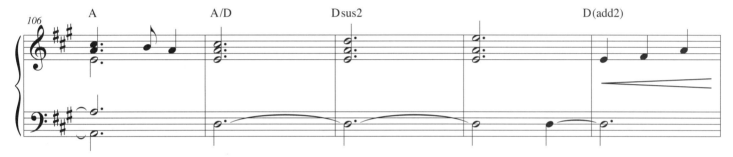

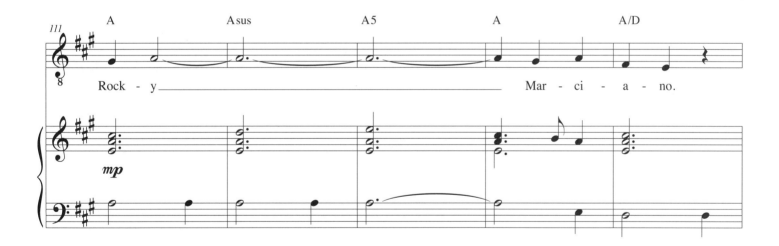

Rock - y _____ Mar - ci - a - no.

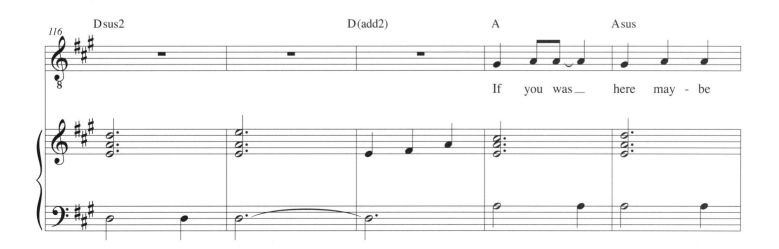

If you was _ here may - be

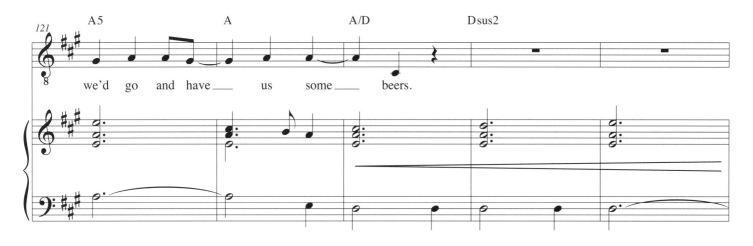

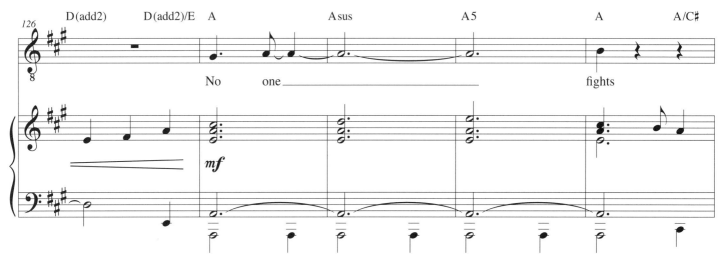

IN THE RING

Lyrics by LYNN AHRENS
Music by STEPHEN FLAHERTY

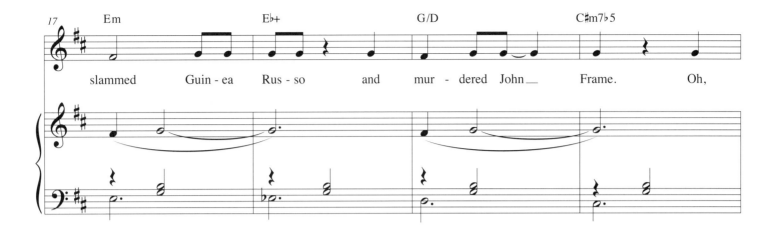

slammed Guin-ea Rus-so and mur-dered John___ Frame. Oh,

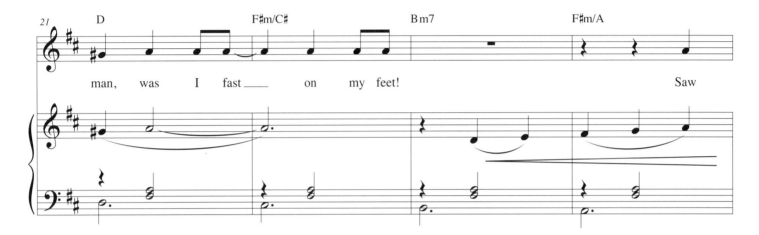

man, was I fast___ on my feet! Saw

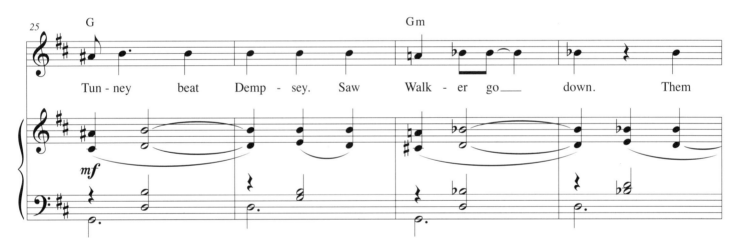

Tun-ney beat Demp-sey. Saw Walk-er go___ down. Them

times was a beau-ti-ful___ thing! The

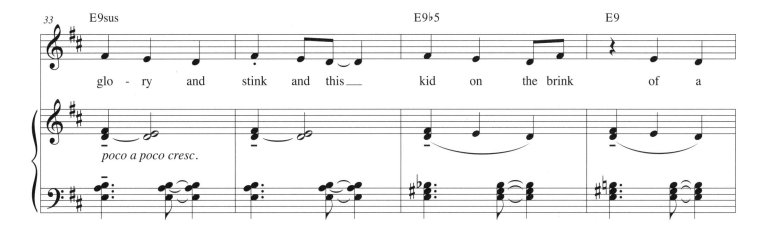

glo - ry and stink and this__ kid on the brink of a

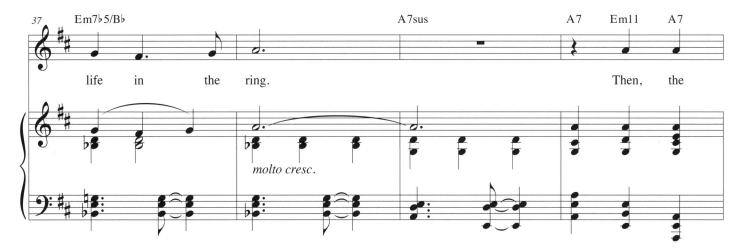

life in the ring. Then, the

coun - try went__ bust. We was hun - gry all__ right. But

I had two fists I could use.__ They'd

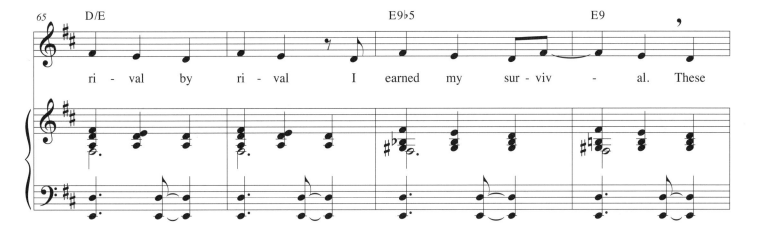

ri - val by ri - val I earned my sur - viv - al. These

scars I got giv - en for liv - in' my life in the

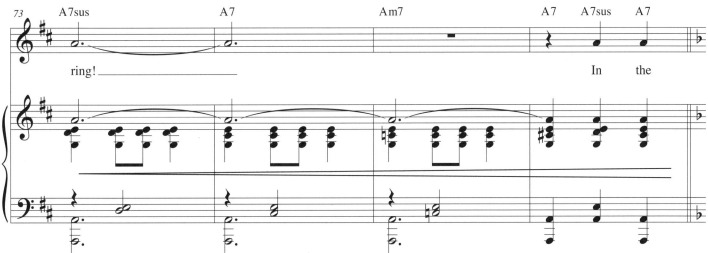

ring! In the

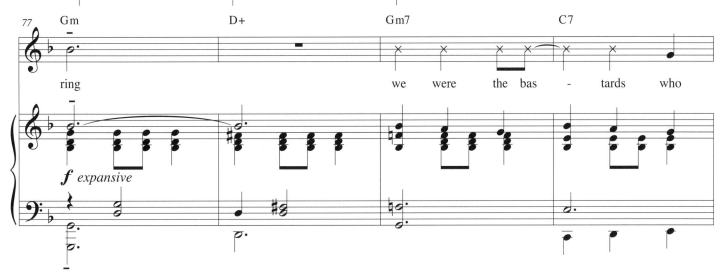

ring we were the bas - tards who

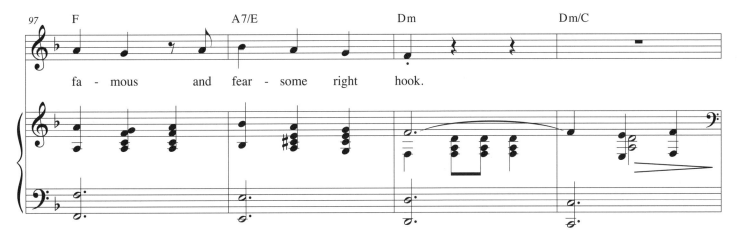

fa - mous and fear - some right hook.

More troubled

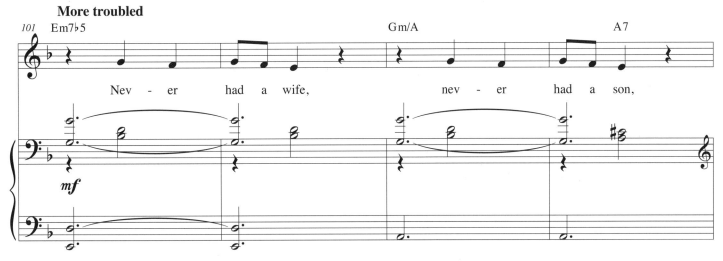

Nev - er had a wife, nev - er had a son,

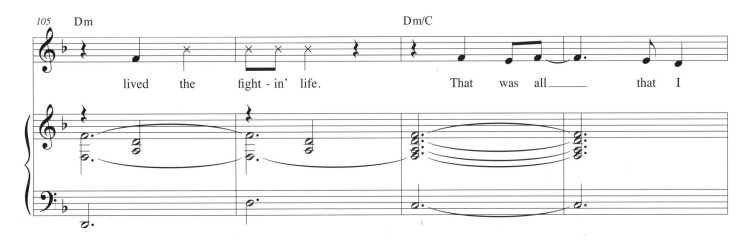

lived the fight - in' life. That was all_____ that I

done. All I

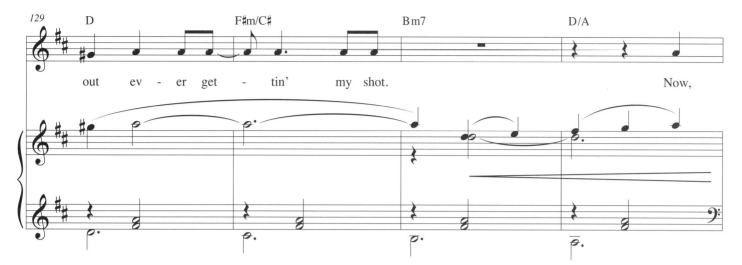

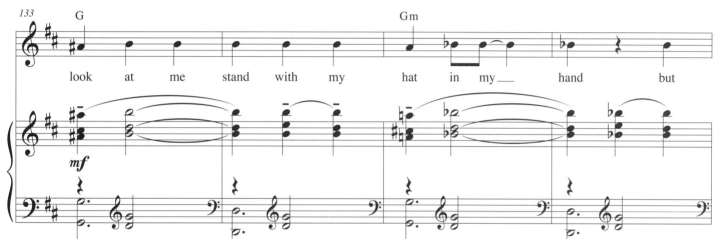

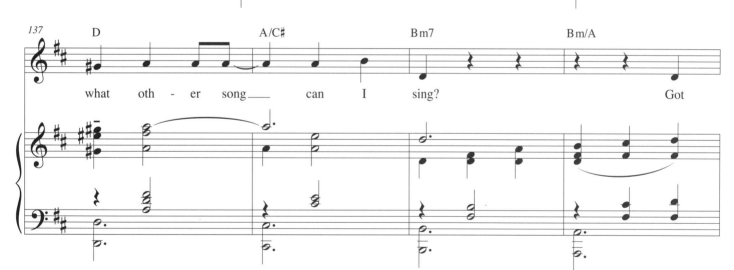

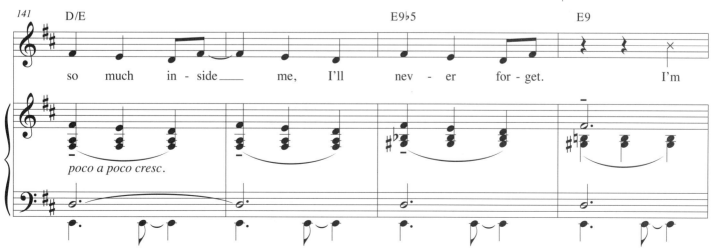

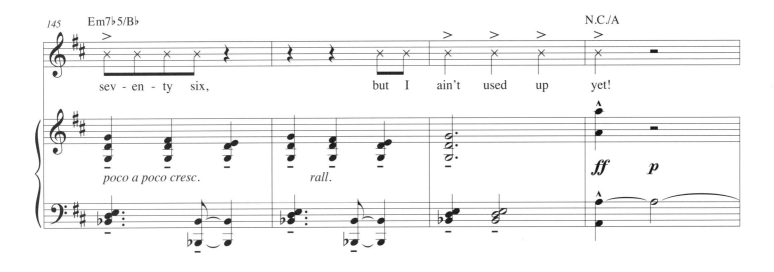

sev - en - ty six, but I ain't used up yet!

poco a poco cresc. rall.

ff p

A bit slower than tempo primo

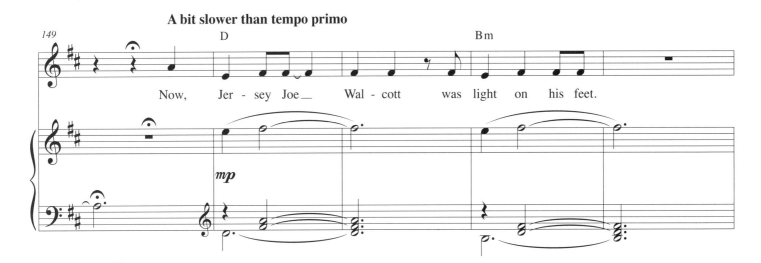

Now, Jer - sey Joe__ Wal - cott was light on his feet.

mp

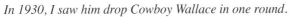

In 1930, I saw him drop Cowboy Wallace in one round. *The way he moved, the man was like...*

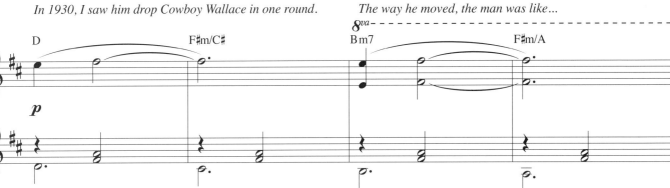

p

...the Fred Astaire of the ring.

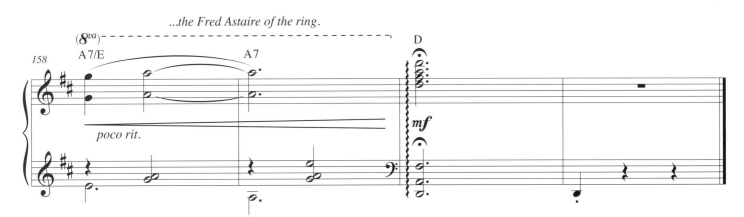

poco rit. mf

HAPPINESS

Lyrics by LYNN AHRENS
Music by STEPHEN FLAHERTY

ROCKY: So here's what it is. Here's how it feels.
ADRIAN:
BOTH: Hav-in' a life with you in it.
ROCKY: Tak-in' it slow.
ADRIAN: Hold-in' my breath.
BOTH: Don't wan-na go and ru-in it. I'm look-in' for words

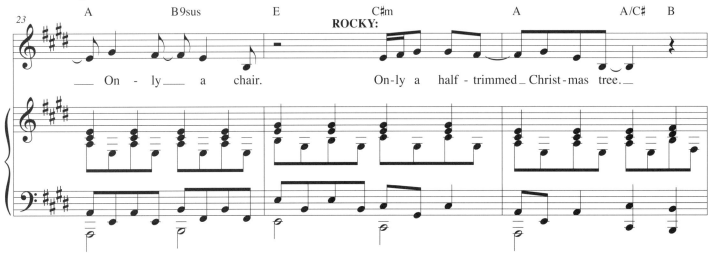

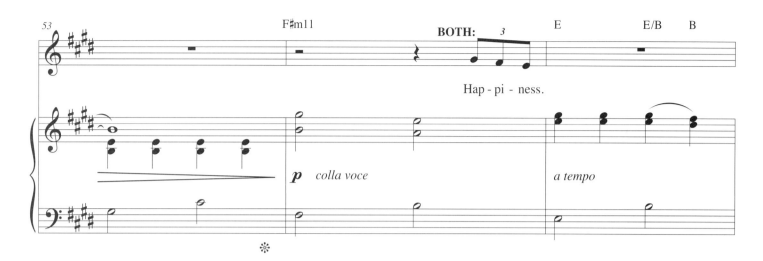

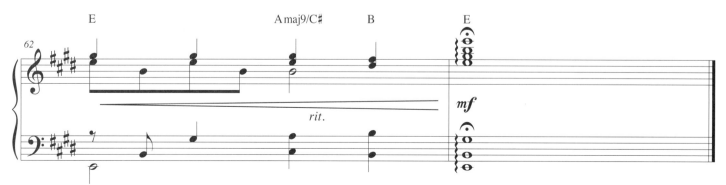

I'M DONE

Lyrics by LYNN AHRENS
Music by STEPHEN FLAHERTY

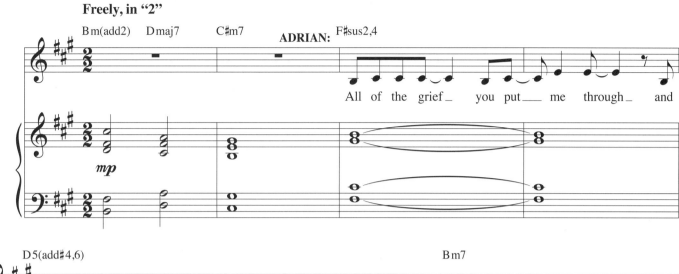

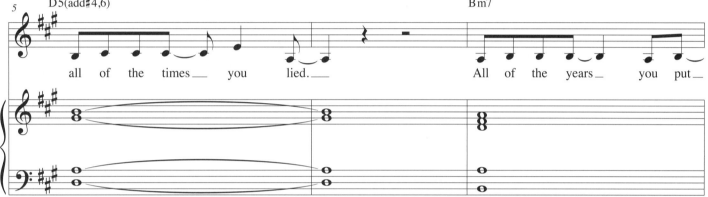

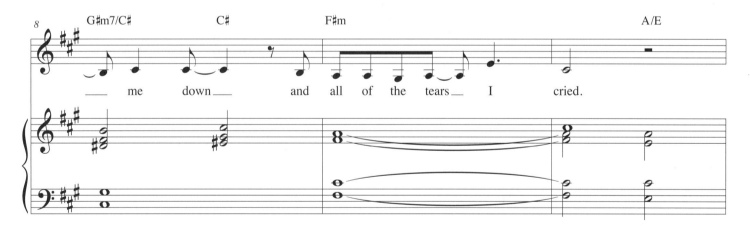

Starkly, emotional

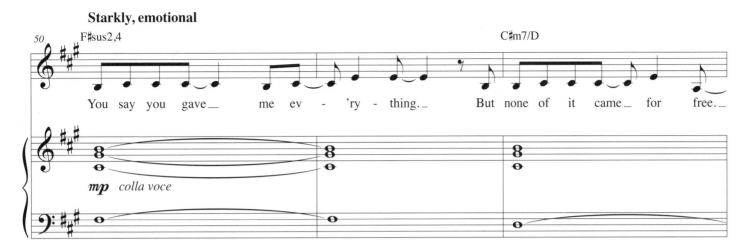

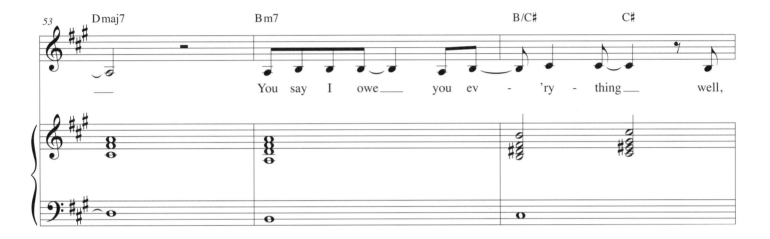

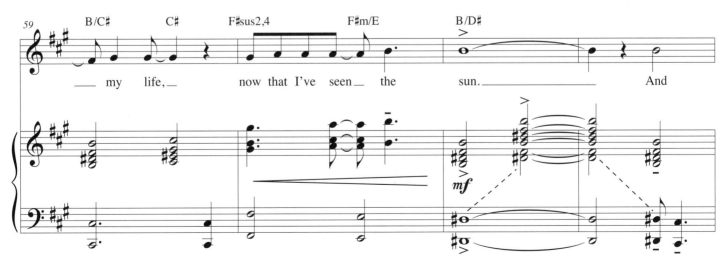

KEEP ON STANDING

Lyrics by LYNN AHRENS
Music by STEPHEN FLAHERTY

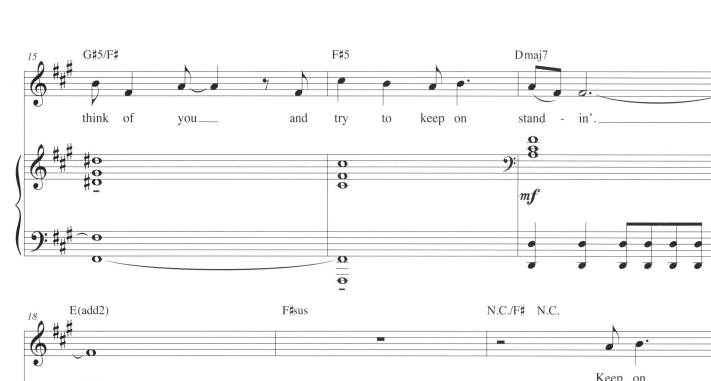

think of you___ and try to keep on stand - in'.___

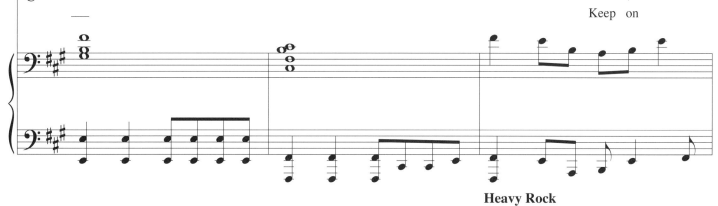

Keep on

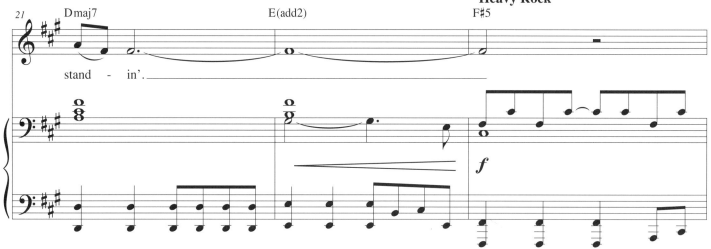

stand - in'.___

Heavy Rock

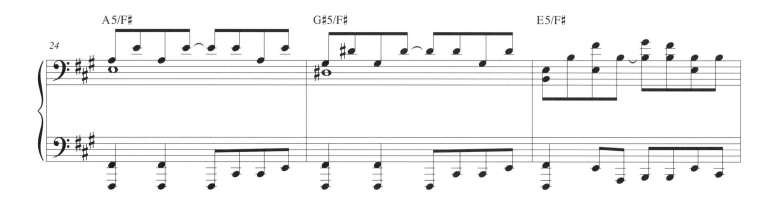

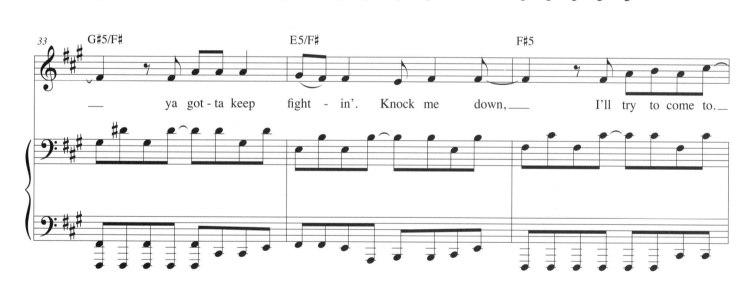

in hell__ I'll win. I know where I'm from.__

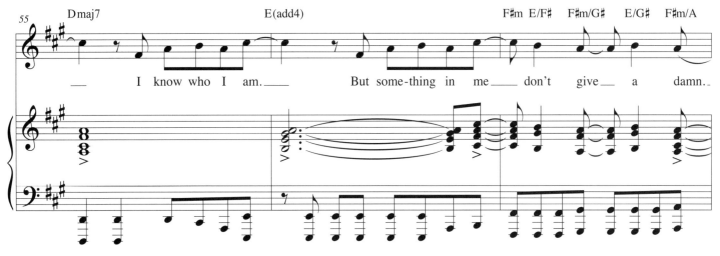

__ I know who I am.__ But some-thing in me__ don't give__ a damn..

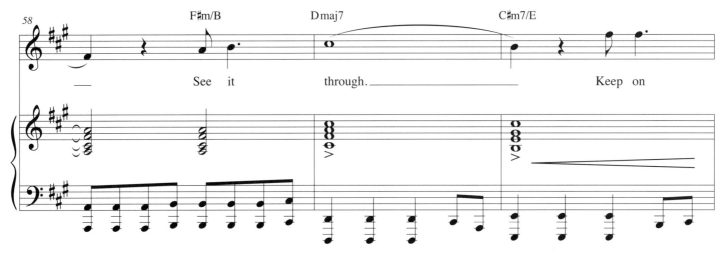

__ See it through.__ Keep on

stand - in'.__

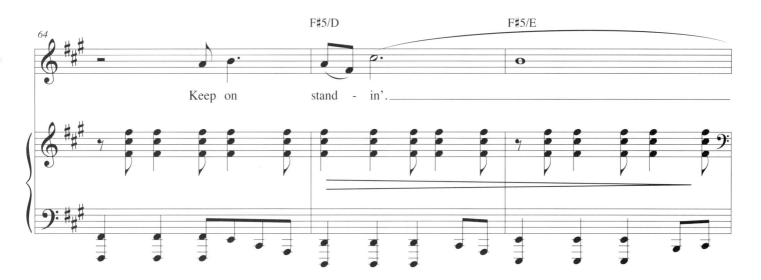

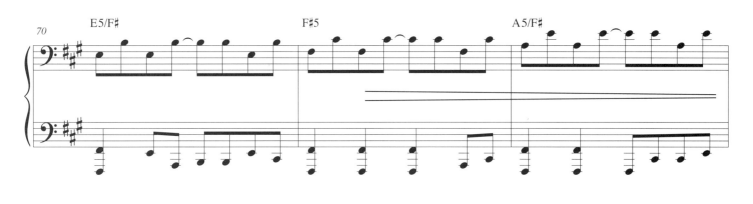

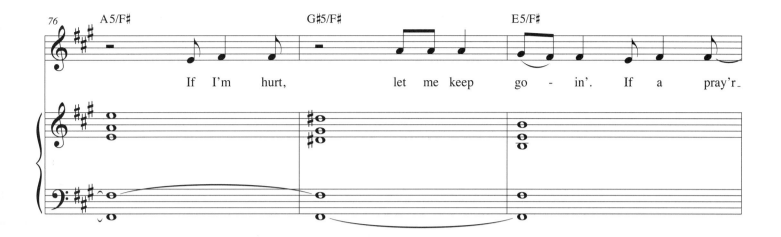

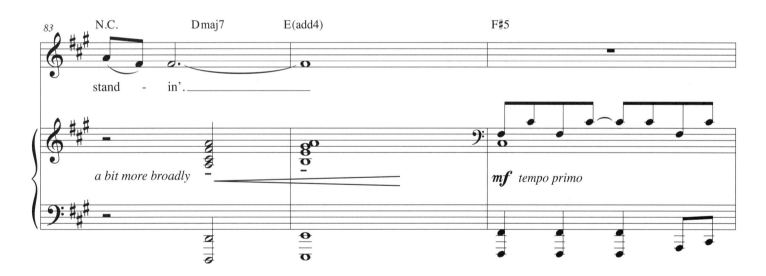

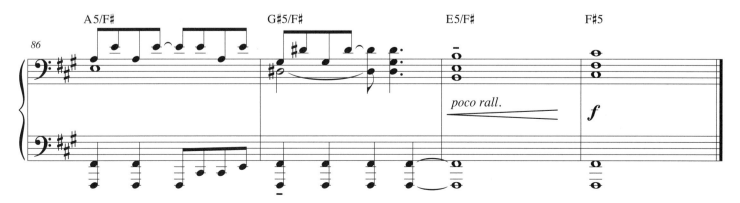